How To Have Sex On Your Birthday

Written By:
Herbert Kavet

Illustrated By:
Martin Riskin

© 1990
by **Ivory Tower Publishing Company, Inc.**
All Rights Reserved

Manufactured in the United States of America

30 29 28 27 26 25 24 23 22 21 20 19 18 17 16 15 14 13 12 11 10 9 8 7 6 5 4

Ivory Tower Publishing Co., Inc.
125 Walnut St., Watertown, MA 02172
Telephone #: (617) 923-1111   Fax #: (617) 923-8839

INTRODUCTION

Sex on your birthday? You bet. What a great way to spend the day or even a few pleasant minutes - if you happen to be over 30 years old. Sex is a splendid idea most any time and on a special day it is a singular pleasure. Since sex usually involves two partners, a certain amount of sharing is necessary. Sometimes the sharing means one partner has to put up with silly costumes, wet rubber duckies or drawn out romantic preparations. But a birthday is a birthday and the birthday girl or boy should be cheerfully indulged on this one day.

SEX
AND
FUN

Sex is fun - right?

It's romantic preparation; it's titillating foreplay; it's ecstatic penetration, surging orgasm and glowing afterplay. It's also sleeping on the wet spot and picking hairs off your tongue. No one writes sonnets about those parts.

SEX
ON YOUR
BIRTHDAY

On your birthday, your partner (or partners for a very lucky few) should conspire to make the sex great and totally satisfying by totally fulfilling all your most ridiculous fantasies and desires.

Read on to learn how.

SEX AS A PRESENT

1. It's less fattening and if done properly much more fun than most chocolate creations.

2. Sex can be done over and over again and if well lubricated it doesn't wear out.

3. Sex doesn't dominate your life as a pet might.

4. It rarely comes in a size you can't use.

SEX
AS A
PRESENT

FINDING A SEX PARTNER

Say you don't get "Sex" as one of your birthday presents. Say you have to find your own sex. What do you do then? Much too much fuss has been made over the difficulty of finding sex. The question is basically simple.

1. You must look in the right places

2. You must resign yourself to doing it alone.

FINDING A SEX PARTNER

To find a perfect partner, what you should look for is someone only slightly hornier than you. Persons more interested in sex than yourself are called perverts.

To find someone slightly hornier than you (if that's possible - I've heard what kind of people read these books), try places where that kind of person is likely to hang out.

Laundromats   Inner City Shelters
Nude Beaches   Crowded Elevators
Maximum Security Prisons   Crack Houses

If you have any luck, let me know 'cause I haven't had any sex on my birthday in 5 years.

SEX
BY YOURSELF

Disadvantages: Loss of eyesight
Risk of growing hair on palms
Pimples

Advantages: You don't have to get all
dressed up to do it.

SEX
BY YOURSELF

To enhance your solo sex, you probably need an inflatable Mr. or Ms. Wonderful that vibrates and pumps in a wild frenzy of passion with life-like soft skin and all sorts of openings and protrusions. Most support up to 250 lbs. and if your weight is in this range, it's no wonder you're alone on your birthday.

TECHNIQUES
FOR FINDING A
SEX PARTNER

O.K. You've already gone to all the single's spots in your area and all the seedy pickup places and still you can't find a partner. At times like this, you need the 5 Secret Never Fail Techniques.

5
SECRET NEVER FAIL TECHNIQUES

1. Personal ads making reference to very large sums of money.

2. Personal ads making reference to very large body parts.

3. Any reference to large body parts.

4. Promising to do a sex act that has never been done to them before.

5. Promising never to tell about it.

ALTERNATIVES TO SEX ON YOUR BIRTHDAY

On so many birthdays, there are disappointments: a pony that never materialized, the sports car that was only a dream, the diamond that turned out to be a fake. In the unlikely event you are so hopeless that even our 5 Secret Never Fail Techniques failed, you need not despair entirely.

There are alternatives to sex.

ALTERNATIVES TO SEX

FOR MEN

World series tickets
Samuel Adams beer and
real salty pretzels
Porsche roadsters
Waterfront property
Dove Bars

FOR WOMEN

Nieman Marcus
Godiva chocolates
Full length coats from only
slightly endangered species
Waterfront property
Ben & Jerry's coffee heath
bar crunch ice cream

FOREPLAY ON YOUR BIRTHDAY

Foreplay is one of the main reasons men and women are called opposite sexes. Men get ready for sex quickly. Most feel the act of unzipping the fly is reasonably sufficient fore-play; especially if they have spent the previous half hour staring at their partner's boobs. Women, most often, are slower to become aroused and prefer a little more tenderness, patience and romance.

FOREPLAY ON YOUR BIRTHDAY

A man will, however, spend extraordinary lengths of time trying to impress a new partner. The lucky woman will be overwhelmed with the most prolonged and imaginative foreplay. Getting back to birthdays, it seems only fair that the birthday boy or girl can call the shots on this one day.

MAN'S BIRTHDAY FOREPLAY		WOMAN'S BIRTHDAY FOREPLAY	
With wife:	17 1/2 seconds	With husband:	45 minutes
With girlfriend:	74 seconds	With boyfriend:	1 1/2 hours
With someone else's wife:	1 1/2 hours (let's see her husband match that)	With someone else's husband:	32 seconds (you can never tell when the kids will get home)

SPECIAL BIRTHDAY SEX POSITIONS

1. POSITION OF THE MELTED CANDLE

Woman on floor, man hanging over edge of bed.

2. BIRTHDAY CAKE EXTRAVAGANZA

Cake crumbs in a nookie, who gets to lick them out?

SPECIAL BIRTHDAY SEX POSITIONS

3. PIN THE TAIL ON THE DONKEY

Husband watching Super Bowl, wife in barn with donkey.

4. BIRTHDAY NOISEMAKER

Party horn where it doesn't belong. Partner tooting a tune.

ERECTIONS
ON YOUR
BIRTHDAY

Men should be allowed all the erections they like on their birthdays. This includes erections in usually embarrassing locations such as nude beaches and locker rooms after a round of golf with the boys. On this one day of the year, they should not have to worry about covering this fine expression of their manhood with a folded newspaper or baggy trousers.

WOMEN AND ERECTIONS

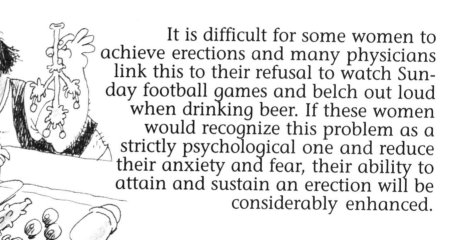

It is difficult for some women to achieve erections and many physicians link this to their refusal to watch Sunday football games and belch out loud when drinking beer. If these women would recognize this problem as a strictly psychological one and reduce their anxiety and fear, their ability to attain and sustain an erection will be considerably enhanced.

HOW TO KEEP YOUR BIRTHDAY ERECTION

I have absolutely no experience with the problem, but I can't help but notice all those ugly stories in the women's magazines. To have a properly celebrated party the birthday boy should keep his erection as long as possible. How do you keep a birthday erection? How? How? I'll tell you how. You tie it to a Q-tip like on all the other days!

PLACES TO KEEP YOUR BIRTHDAY ERECTION

Should you have to temporarily cover a birthday erection due to the proximity of some priggish intruders, here are 4 Standard Techniques.

1. You can bury it in the ground by lying on your stomach.

2. You can hide it behind a folded and discretely carried newspaper.

3. You can lose it in a pair of really baggy trousers.

4. You can do as some of us must and coil the offending member around and around your body pretending any excess hanging out is a fire hose.

THE BIRTHDAY FART

On this one day of the year, it is totally acceptable to break wind in public without being considered an ill-mannered barbarian. You can break wind in private, like everyone else of course, to your heart's content during the rest of the year.

THE BIRTHDAY FART

When you fart on your birthday no one will turn a head, make faces or expressions of disgust or inquire as to the condition of your intestinal track. In really sophisticated company, you may even receive a little polite applause.

ORGASMS
ON YOUR
BIRTHDAY

Everyone having sex on their birthday is entitled to one (at least) really intense orgasm. O.K., you say, but how do I find this kind of exquisite orgasm?

You find one by finding a partner who is imaginative, thoughtful, considerate, romantic, attractive and willing to get into bed with you.

Good luck.

GREAT ORGASMS REQUIRE A WILLING PARTNER

Your partner must be willing, above all, to let you reach your birthday orgasm before rolling over and going to sleep.

HOW TO TELL WHEN YOU'VE HAD YOUR BIRTHDAY ORGASM

Sometimes it's hard to tell when your partner (or in some cases yourself) has had The Birthday Orgasm. This lack of knowledge can lead to wasted time, useless exertion, unnecessary wear and tear on your playpen and unpleasant chaffing. All these problems are avoided if you know exactly when your partner is done.

HOW TO TELL WHEN YOUR PARTNER HAS HAD A BIRTHDAY ORGASM

WOMEN

1. Sometimes they will let you know by screaming I'm coming, I'm coming or Ohmygod, Ohmygod.

2. Sometimes they will shudder and moan and snuggle nicely as close as possible to you causing a limb to deaden and turn green with gangrene.

3. Most often they will just keep going until parts of your anatomy go numb or minor bleeding (yours) starts to stain the sheets.

MEN

1. If it's not your first date with the guy, he will immediately roll over and go to sleep.

DESCRIBING YOUR BIRTHDAY ORGASM

Say you want to tell all your friends about your birthday orgasm the next day but you find your everyday vocabulary just doesn't seem adequate. We can help. Just pick a word from column A and combine it with one from B and C. The whole gang will know exactly what you are trying to say.

DESCRIBING YOUR
BIRTHDAY
ORGASM

A.

Pre-eminent
Magnificent
Perfect
Stupendous
Princely
Exorbitant
Scrumptious
Gorgeous
Beauteous
Preposterous

B.

Trembling
Cracking
Vibrating
Squirming
Throbbing
Exploding
Bursting
Roaring
Detonating
Fizzling

C.

Ejaculation
Physical
Shoot Off
Climax
Erruption
Buzz
Come
Pop
Blast
Misfire

FAKING ORGASM
ON YOUR
BIRTHDAY

MEN

Maybe you're tired. Maybe you gave at the office. Maybe worries and pressures prevent you from achieving your birthday orgasm. Rather than have your partner feel she has failed you, it's probably a lot simpler to just fake an orgasm.

FAKING ORGASM
ON YOUR
BIRTHDAY

MEN

Faking an orgasm by men is usually considered to be very difficult. Not so. It can be accomplished by anyone with moderate dexterity if the room is kept in darkness, the partner rather inexperienced and a small glass of some warm liquid kept handy.

FAKING ORGASM
ON YOUR
BIRTHDAY

WOMEN

All women take a course in their last year of high school that teaches them how to fake orgasms. The course often carries a name like Home Economics, Physical Education or Women Problems to fool the male gym teachers. No male is ever allowed to attend these classes.

FAKING ORGASM
ON YOUR
BIRTHDAY

WOMEN

The usual 120 hours of instruction in these fake orgasm classes includes screaming, thrashing about, sighing, moaning, scratching and uninhibited use of obscenities. A passing grade is required before any of the girls are allowed to have sex.

SIMULTANEOUS ORGASMS ON YOUR BIRTHDAY

When you and your partner have the same birthday what better way to celebrate than with simultaneous orgasms. Simultaneous orgasms you say? I hear that's really hard to carry off. Perhaps for some, but not for those familiar with the 5 hard and fast rules for simultaneous orgasm.

RULES FOR SIMULTANEOUS ORGASMS

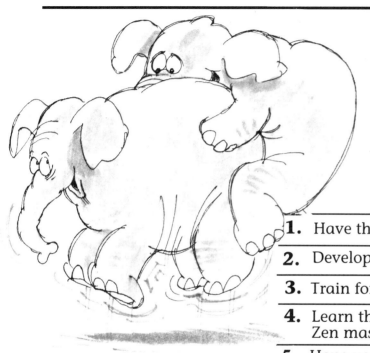

1. Have the patience of a saint.

2. Develop the timing of a John McEnroe.

3. Train for the endurance of an iron man triathlon.

4. Learn the concentration and the mind control of a Zen master.

5. Hope you are a very lucky person because with all of the above your chances are still only 1 in 100 that the two of you will still be on speaking terms by the time you work this one out.

ROMANTIC SEX ON YOUR BIRTHDAY

Sometimes a birthday person, often a woman, yearns for romantic sex on her birthday. Romantic sex is easy if you just follow these 7 simple steps.

1. Feather your love nest with care and capitalize on all your partner's secret idiosyncrasies.

2. Don't rush the foreplay.

3. Make the initial penetration a tantillizingly slow process.

ROMANTIC SEX ON YOUR BIRTHDAY

4. Strive for simultaneous orgasm.

5. Strive for multiple orgasm.

6. Dawdle over the afterplay.

7. Never, never leave any cash on the pillow.

MULTIPLE ORGASMS ON YOUR BIRTHDAY

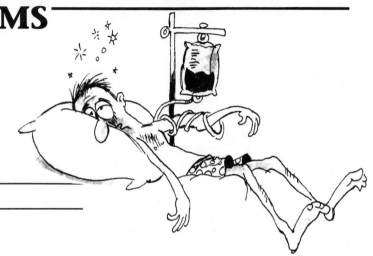

If A Man

1. Be under 19 years of age.

If A Woman

1. Find a man under 19 years old.

2. Teach him to slow down.

MULTIPLE ORGASMS ON YOUR BIRTHDAY

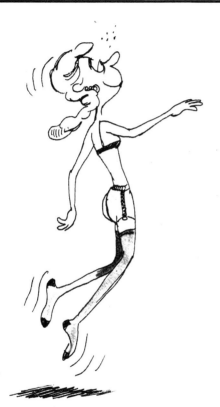

If A Woman

3. Stimulate his competitive spirit with vague references to other lovers who were absolutely sensational.

4. Direct him carefully using simple 2 syllable words like higher, lower, softer, harder, faster.

5. Never be embarrassed about using a good vibrator.

BIRTH CONTROL ON YOUR BIRTHDAY

Whatever you do, don't skimp on birth control for your birthday. Avoid problems and do it right. Remember the fellow who was so cheap he had his vasectomy done at Sears. Every time he got an erection the garage door went up.

BIRTH CONTROL ON YOUR BIRTHDAY

Condoms are the fun sex product of the 90's. You can even change the color of your penis with a condom allowing a partner to experiment with interracial sex without upsetting neighbors or parents. Glow in the dark condoms are even available to help see where to put "it" in dim light.

KINKY SEX ON YOUR BIRTHDAY

Not every sex partner wants to get involved with rubber sheets, baby oil, tingly cold chains, leather underwear and feathery duck suits. Still, a birthday is a birthday and a special day and the birthday girl or boy should be able to get a few innocent perversions satisfied.

INTRODUCING YOUR PARTNER TO KINKY SEX

It is natural to be shy about sharing your fantasies and kinky obsessions even with a birthday partner. Still, to insure a rich, full, stimulating birthday, you'll have to bring the little idiosyncrasies out of the closet, you weird devil you.

The three steps:

1. Talk about it realistically, maturely, and with dignity.

2. Calm his or her shrieking while you explain why the rubber sheets, enema, ducky and zucchini are really necessary for your total fulfillment.

3. Resign yourself to having all your partner's friends refer to you for the rest of your life as a weirdo.

GOING TOO FAR

Yes, indeed, you are both consenting adults, and you agreed to try one of your fantasy sex scenarios.

You've gone too far if:

1. Your partner faints.

2. Your partner gags.

3. Your partner leaves you.

4. Your partner physically attacks you. (unless that is part of your fantasy).

5. Your partner starts to enjoy it more than you do.

HOW TO CALM A HORRIFIED PARTNER

First, calmly put away the oils, the rubber, the vibrator, the leather, the crotchless panties and all the other sex aids. Then decide which of the three guaranteed methods of calming a horrified partner you will use.

The three methods:

1. Forget it. "O.K., we tried it and you didn't like it. We'll forget it."

2. Modify it. "How about we'll use a smaller vibrator and less ice in the peanut oil."

3. Repeat it. "We'll just give it another chance. I'm sure you'll get used to it.

None of these work.

SEX PROBLEMS ON YOUR BIRTHDAY

Premature Ejaculation

Premature ejaculation is not exactly a problem. I mean if it's your birthday and that's your thing, who has the right to complain. If it's your partner's birthday, of course, and all the excitement sort of over stimulates you, well that's a cause for bitching. Some people have even been known to have their sexual impulses triggered by those feathery party favors that unroll when you blow them. I mean talk about leaving a partner unfulfilled.

HOW TO CURE PREMATURE EJACULATION

Women rarely have a problem with premature ejaculation. Men can find a cure in the birthday celebration itself. A little vanilla ice cream, or some favorite flavor rubbed on the offending member should dampen a persons ardor enough to permit more sustained sexual activity.

IMPOTENCE
ON YOUR
BIRTHDAY

MEN

The chief cause of impotence among men on birthdays as well as most other days is tricky bra straps. The top hook or two on these devilish devices have been designed to rehook themselves when you go onto the lower catches. This makes casual and romantic removal by a man impossible. The only way a man can possibly unhook a bra is to place the woman face down on a firm working surface and use both hands and full concentration. Who can blame the fellow for losing interest by this point.

The cure for male impotence is simply to have the woman remove the bra by herself. Any female can easily accomplish this with one hand.

IMPOTENCE
ON YOUR
BIRTHDAY

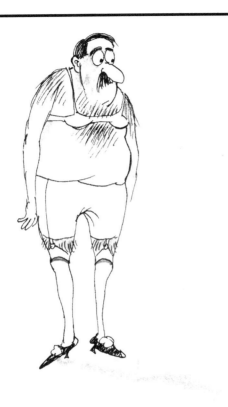

WOMEN

No one knows the cause of
impotence in women.

ONE SIZE FITS ALL PANTYHOSE AND YOUR BIRTHDAY

There is a story about an amorous young couple who made enthusiastic and energetic love. As the two fell back satiated, the young man felt some pangs of guilt at his barely controlled enthusiasm and apologized. "I'm terribly sorry, but if I knew you were a virgin I would have taken more time". The girl quickly responded, "If I knew we had more time, I would have taken off my pantyhose".

PANTYHOSE AND SEX

The problem with pantyhose is that after they are pulled down a foot or two and a bit of the necessary machinery is exposed, an average lover thinks the job is complete. Ho Ho Ho. Just at that point the stuff tangles around her (or his) knees and it's like trying to have sex with rubber bands holding your thighs together.

FRIGIDITY ON A BIRTHDAY

There are two theories on frigidity. One holds that there are no frigid women only awkward men. The other talks about a wife so frigid that when she spreads her legs, the furnace goes on.

Main Causes of Frigidity

1. Partner keeps asking how long you are going to take.

2. You keep hearing your mother calling.

CAUSES OF FRIGIDITY

3. Partner calls you by the wrong name.

4. You can't remember your partner's name.

5. You are afraid of someone coming into the room, especially your husband.

6. Partner's religious medallion keeps banging you in the nose.

10
GREAT
SEX GAMES
FOR YOUR
BIRTHDAY

1. Gladiator and The Slave Girl

2. Ooh, Mr. Iceman

3. Rubber Band Bondage

4. Plumbers Have Long Plungers

5. Whipped Cream Swimming Pool

GREAT SEX GAMES FOR YOUR BIRTHDAY

6. Lashed with Wet Linguini

7. Venetion Night with the Hardy Boatman

8. Spanked and Ravished in the Sultan Harem

9. Leather Undies Model

10. Massage Your What?

HAVING AN ORGY ON YOUR BIRTHDAY

An orgy can be a wonderful way to cele-brate your birthday. But how can I start an orgy? you say. The secret to starting an orgy is to have lots of horny friends. Actu-ally, almost everybody seems to have lots of horny friends. The problem is that all of them are the same sex as you. This makes for a very dull orgy unless you are a homosexual and homosexuals, as everyone knows, have orgies all the time anyhow.

Once you have an orgy going, you'll have no trouble continuing it and having a fas-cinating time. It's getting them started that is the tough part and I haven't the foggiest idea of how to get them started.

HOW TO HAVE AN ORGY ON YOUR BIRTHDAY

Getting an orgy started is the hard part!

SAFE SEX ON YOUR BIRTHDAY

Safe sex is as important on your birthday as it is on Friday nights.

Safe Sex Is:

Old Fashioned Girdles
Stuck Zippers
A Partner With A Bad Headache
Spreading Cases Of Poison Ivy

SAFE SEX ON YOUR BIRTHDAY

Safe Sex Is:

A Woman Who Changes Her Mind
Donations To A Sperm Bank
Talking Dirty On The Phone
Jealous Pets

IMAGINATIVE PLACES TO HAVE BIRTHDAY SEX

Excitement may be waning if your birthday celebration takes place in the same bed where 98% of your regular sex takes place. For a spirited and carefree birthday use some imagination.

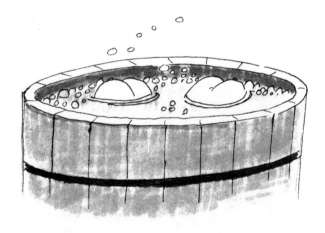

IMAGINATIVE PLACES TO HAVE BIRTHDAY SEX

1. In a hot tub.

2. While traveling through a car wash.

3. On a waterbed coated in mineral oil.

4. In a bathtub filled with lumpy oatmeal.

5. Under a blanket on a public beach (taking special care the sand doesn't get you know where).

BIRTHDAY SEX FOR CHUBBY PEOPLE

Chubby people (often enviously called Fat People) should also enjoy sex on their birthdays. The exercise is good for them and the overall act healthy and erotically fulfilling. Really vigorous sex is a fine way to slim thighs and buttocks and can be enjoyed safely if the 5 rules of chubby sex are followed.

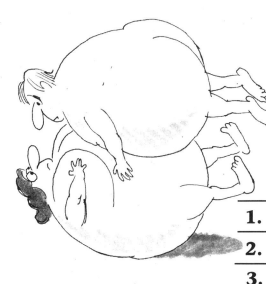

5
RULES OF
CHUBBY SEX

1. Side by side is a lot safer than "on top of".

2. Flimsy beds eventually lead to embarrassment.

3. Catching celullite in a zipper can dampen the most enflamed ardor.

4. The more there is to touch the more there is to turn you on.

5. The bigger you are, the bigger the orgasm.

BIRTHDAY SEX AND CALORIES

Old fashioned birthday parties with ice cream and cake and physical activity limited to "pin the tail on the donkey" can only lead to chubby little birthday girls and boys. Sex on your birthday, however, not only burns loads of calories but if done correctly, will definitely improve your aerobic capacity.

ACTIVITY	CALORIES BURNED
Finding a birthday sex partner:	
a. If you're a virile, handsome, or voluptuous beauty	75 calories
b. Rest of us.	468 calories

BIRTHDAY SEX AND CALORIES

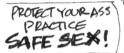 

PROTECT YOUR ASS PRACTICE SAFE SEX!

AIDS AND YOUR WEENIE!

DON'T DO IT IF YOU... HAVEN'T PUT ONE ON!

ACTIVITY	CALORIES BURNED
Worrying about safe sex:	
a. If single	75 calories
b. If married	
with wife	2 calories
with someone else's wife	150 calories
with stranger	1063 calories

BIRTHDAY SEX AND CALORIES

ACTIVITY	CALORIES CONSUMED
Presents	
a. Opening presents	20 calories
b. Opening presents while making love	65 calories
c. Hiding another lover's present while making love	180 calories
Singing Happy Birthday	
a. While holding a cake	15 calories
b. While making love	65 calories
c. While performing an oral sex act	290 calories

BIRTHDAY SEX AND CALORIES

ACTIVITY	CALORIES BURNED
Sex Fantasies	
a. Talking partner into fantasy	350 calories
b. Gathering paraphernalia for fantasy	162 calories
c. Acting out fantasy	75 calories
d. Acting out fantasy that doesn't work	770 calories
e. Calming horrified partner afterwards.	400 calories
f. Putting up with ridicule	25 calories

BIRTHDAY SEX AND CALORIES

ACTIVITY	CALORIES BURNED
Premature ejaculation	
a. If a man	2 calories
b. Explanation by man	163 calories
c. If a woman	280 calories
d. Horny woman	680 calories
Impotence	
a. If a man - first time	160 calories
b. If a man - second time	1620 calories
Frigidity	
a. If a woman with a headache	1 calories
b. If a man who thought this was a sure thing	50 calories
c. If a man who thought this was a sure thing and already bragged to friends	260 calories

BIRTHDAY SEX AND CALORIES

ACTIVITY	CALORIES BURNED
Removing bra	
a. If a woman	5 calories
b. If a man	105 calories
c. If a man in the heat of passion	350 calories
d. If a man in the heat of passion with one hand	2372 calories
Removing pantyhose	
a. If a woman	10 calories
b. If a man	125 calories
c. Forgetting to remove pantyhose	830 calories

FREQUENTLY ASKED QUESTIONS DURING BIRTHDAY SEX

People probably ask far too many questions during sexual activities which is a pretty good indication of just how insecure they are about these things. At a time when a few words of tender love are called for, people say things like:

Is it in?(particularly daunting to a man's ardor)

Was it O.K. for you too?

Are you done yet?

You're done already?

Do you love me?

FREQUENTLY ASKED QUESTIONS DURING BIRTHDAY SEX

Can I come now?

Are my elbows bleeding?

Must you do that?

Why won't you do it?

Do you often do this sort of thing?

THE CONSIDERATE BIRTHDAY LOVER

1. Always lets the birthday person climax first.

2. Never comes to bed with cold hands or feet.

3. Volunteers to sleep on the wet spot.

4. Never leans on a limb until it becomes numb.

5. Is not distraught if you fart under the covers.

THE CONSIDERATE BIRTHDAY LOVER

6. Gives hard or tickly back rubs as desired.

7. Never glances at the T.V. even if it's a championship game.

8. Convinces you it was their greatest experience ever.

9. Is always willing to keep going even if they'll be sore for a week.

10. Never makes a face during oral sex.

GUIDE TO SEX AIDS FOR BIRTHDAY PRESENTS

Sex aids make a thoughtful and titillating birthday gift. The nice U.P.S. man in his or her brown suit will be happy to deliver them directly to your front door. U.P.S. people are always running because they know how anxious you are for those plain unmarked packages.

Vibrators

Contrary to all the ads these are not used to soothe sore muscles but to make your erogenous zones go ZZZZZZ.

GUIDE TO SEX AIDS FOR BIRTHDAY PRESENTS

Oils, Lotions & Lubricants

These are all colorless, tasteless and non-irritating, unless you want to buy the kind that are and that help you to slide around on a waterbed or your partner. Don't forget to wash off both afterwards.

Life Size Dolls

For men and women, with built in vibrators and everything. I suspect by the time you inflate one of these things you are good for nothing else that day.

Ben Wa Balls

No Westerner has any idea what to do with these.

HOW TO HAVE SEX ON YOUR **BIRTHDAY** AND STILL BE A **VIRGIN**

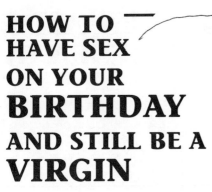

There are lots of ways to enjoy the fun of sex and still retain your virginity. Check out the following list:

You're still a virgin if ...

It's too dark to see very much

Your date had a vasectomy

You've had a little too much to drink

It's not a meaningful relationship

HOW TO HAVE SEX ON YOUR BIRTHDAY AND STILL BE A VIRGIN

You're still a virgin if ...

It was sort of a favor for an old friend
The earth didn't shake and wobble
You forgot your partner's name
You're on vacation

THE MISSIONARY POSITION ON YOUR BIRTHDAY

What's wrong with the good old missionary position for your birthday?

Man on Top

Woman on Bottom

THE MISSIONARY POSITION ON YOUR BIRTHDAY

Standard Missionary Position:
Man on mission to meet sales quota. Woman in bed with doorman.

Liberated Missionary Position:
Woman on top. Man doing dishes.

Kinky Missionary Position:
Woman on top of refrigerator. Man with thighs in ice cube tray.

Oral Missionary Position:
Woman on bottom. Man licks icing off birthday cake.

INTIMATE APPAREL FOR BIRTHDAY PRESENTS

Do you want some sexy intimate apparel instead of perfume, candy or ties for your birthday? Well, it pays to advertise. Take a look on the next page and put a discrete check next to the item that turns you on. Leave the list in a place it will be seen.

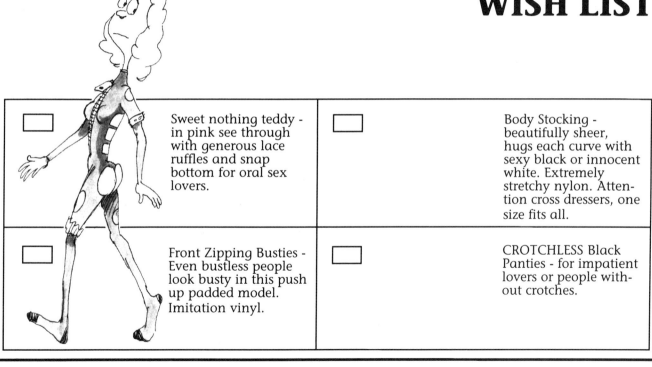

BIRTHDAY INTIMATE APPAREL WISH LIST

☐ Sweet nothing teddy - in pink see through with generous lace ruffles and snap bottom for oral sex lovers.

☐ Body Stocking - beautifully sheer, hugs each curve with sexy black or innocent white. Extremely stretchy nylon. Attention cross dressers, one size fits all.

☐ Front Zipping Busties - Even bustless people look busty in this push up padded model. Imitation vinyl.

☐ CROTCHLESS Black Panties - for impatient lovers or people without crotches.

BIRTHDAY VASECTOMY

Whose birthday is it anyhow?
I for one have forbidden the
word to be mentioned in my
house.

BIRTHDAY CIRCUMCISION

A liberated woman's group whose name will be left un-mentioned have announced that they are trying to stop the circumcision of men. They found they were throwing away the best part.

BIRTHDAY SEX FOR THE WELL ENDOWED

Well endowed women and men
are wonderful people to enjoy
birthday sex with.

Advantages of Being Well Endowed

1. You get the most out of a stretch fabric.

2. You can keep magazines dry in the bathtub.

3. You have a great place to hang towels or look for lost earrings.

ADVANTAGES OF BEING WELL ENDOWED

4. You make jogging a spectator sport.

5. You need much less push when doing push ups.

6. You are seldom lonely at a beach.

7. You meet lots of cute doctors and nurses when you get caught in zippers.

SEX ON SPECIAL BIRTHDAYS

The "0" birthdays have always been special. Those are the times you get the surprise parties, the office celebration and the expensive presents.

30
Year Olds

You start wearing underwear almost all the time.

Try having 30 orgasms that week or if that's too many, how about 30 minutes of talking dirty.

SEX ON SPECIAL BIRTHDAYS

40
Year Olds

You feel like the morning after and you can swear you haven't been anywhere.

Do it for 40 minutes in a hammock without falling out. Do it for 40 minutes period, without falling out.

50
Year Olds

You don't care where your wife goes when she goes out as long as you don't have to go with her.

Two 25 year olds are always nice.

60
Year Olds

It takes you all night to do what you used to do all night.

Spend 60 minutes relearning foreplay. See if your partner can stay awake that long.

EXCUSES FOR NOT HAVING SEX ON YOUR BIRTHDAY

Sometimes you just might not want to have sex on your birthday. I know it sounds crazy but it does happen to some people. Here's a list of plausible excuses so your partner won't be hurt.

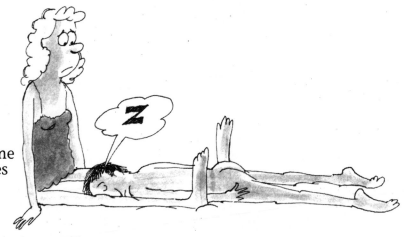

1. I can get it up alright, I'm just tired.

2. I have such a headache, the sound of an erection would split my brain.

EXCUSES FOR NOT HAVING SEX ON YOUR BIRTHDAY

3. Again? We just did it last month.

4. I hardly know you (awkward if married to person).

5. I'm sorry about this bladder infection.

6. It's that time of month again? Again?

RATING YOUR BIRTHDAY SEX

Your Sex Was Great If:

The heat of your passion melted all the candles on your cake.

Your partner surprises you with sex in a hot tub.

Your Sex Was Lousy If:

The heat of all your candles melted the cake.

Your in-laws catch you with the baby sitter on the kitchen table.

RATING YOUR BIRTHDAY SEX

Your Sex Was Great If:

Your lover sings your praise all year long.

Your birthday party degenerates into an orgy.

Your Sex Was Lousy If:

Your lover starts to sing you Happy Birthday but forgets your name.

Your birthday party degenerates into a food fight.

THE 10 COMMANDMENTS

I Thou shall not climax before the birthday boy or girl.

II Thou shalt not skimp on fore-play.

III Thou shalt engage in afterplay before falling asleep.

IV Thou shalt indulge your partner's fantasies no matter how idiotic.

V Thou shalt encourage your partner to experience multiple orgasms.

THE 10 COMMANDMENTS

VI Thou shall not make fun of your partner's shortcomings.

VII Thou shalt search diligently for erogenous zones.

VIII Thou shalt talk or scream or remain silent as the birthday boy or girl wishes.

IX Thou shalt endure uncomfortable positions if they really make your partner happy.

X Thou shalt not talk about the experience with anyone but your very best friends.

You may send directly to us for the books below. Please add $3.00 for shipping and handling.

TRADE PAPERBACK BOOKS $5.95

2400	Sex On Your Birthday
2402	Confessions From Bathroom
2403	Good Bonking Guide
2404	Sex Slave
2405	Mid-Life Sex
2406	World's Sex Records
2407	40: The Big Four-Oh
2408	30: The Big Three-Oh
2409	50: The Big Five-Oh
2411	Geriatric Sex Guide
2412	Golf Shots
2415	Birthdays Happen
2416	Absolutely Worst Fart
2417	Women Over 30 Are Better
2418	9 Months in Sac
2419	Cucumbers Are Better
2421	Honeymoon Guide
2422	Eat Yourself Healthy
2423	Sex After 40?
2424	Sex After 50?
2425	Women Over 40 Are Better
2426	Women Over 50 Are Better
2427	Over The Hill
2428	Beer Is Better
2429	Married to a Computer
2430	Sex After 30?
2431	Happy B'day Old Fart
2432	Big Weenies
2434	Sex And Marriage
2435	Baby's First Year
2436	How To Love A New Yorker
2437	The Retirement Book
2438	Dog Farts
2439	Handling His Mid-Life Crisis
2440	How To Love A Texan
2441	Bedtime Stories...Kitty
2442	Bedtime Stories...Doggie
2443	60 With Sizzle!
2444	The Wedding Night
2445	Woman's Birthday Wish
2446	The PMS Book
2447	The Pregnant Father
2448	Games Play In Bed
2449	The Barf Book
2450	How To Pick Up Girls
2451	How To Pick Up Guys
2452	Driving Amongst Idiots
2453	Beginner's Sex Manual
2454	Get Well
2455	Unspeakably Rotten Cartoons
2456	For A Million Bucks...
2457	Hooters
2458	Adult Connect the Dots
2459	Once Upon A Mattress
2460	Golfing Amongst Idiots
2461	Marry Me, Marry Me
2462	Smokers Are People, Too
2463	Butts & Buns
2464	101 Drinking Games
2465	Do-It-Yourself Guide Safe Sex
2466	A Connoisseur's Guide To Intimate Apparel
2468	Great Proposals
2469	Hunks
2470	How To Find A Man & Get Married In 30 Days

FUN BOOKS $3.00

2026	Games Play In Bed
2034	You're Over 40 When...
2042	Cucumbers Are Better
2064	Wedding Night
2067	It's Time To Retire When...
2068	Sex Manual...Over 30
2102	You're Over 50 When...
2127	Your Golf Game
2131	The Fart Book
2136	The Shit List
2148	Dear Teacher
2166	Survived Catholic School
2177	You're Over The Hill
2180	Italian Sex Manual
2181	Jewish Sex Manual
2192	You're Over 30 When...
2195	Beer Is Better
2203	The Last Fart Book
2205	Sex After 40?
2210	Sex After Marriage?
2213	Women Over 50 Are Better
2217	Sex After 50?
2224	Life's A Picnic...Big Weenie
2225	Women Over 40 Are Better
2226	C.R.S.
2227	Happy Birthday/Year Older
2229	You're A Redneck
2233	Small Busted Women
2234	You're Over 60
2235	You Know You're Over 70
2236	Nose Picker's Guide
2237	55 & Picking Up Speed
2240	Dumb Men Jokes
2241	Cats Are Better Than Men
2242	Working Woman's Doodle
2243	Working Man's Doodle
2244	Words of Wisdom
2245	Potty Potpourri

HARDCOVER BOOKS $8.95

2350	Sailing
2351	Computers
2352	Cats
2353	Tennis
2354	Bowling
2355	Parenting
2356	Fitness
2357	Golf
2358	Fishing
2359	Bathrooms
2360	Biking
2361	Running
2362	Skiing
2363	Doctors
2364	Lawyers
2365	Teachers
2366	Nurses
2367	Firefighters
2368	Marines

Ivory Tower Publishing Co., Inc., 125 Walnut St., P.O. Box 9132, Watertown, MA 02272-9132   Tel: (617) 923-1111